Original title:
Inside the Home of Hope

Copyright © 2025 Creative Arts Management OÜ
All rights reserved.

Author: Matthew Whitaker
ISBN HARDBACK: 978-1-80587-127-9
ISBN PAPERBACK: 978-1-80587-597-0

Glimmers of Tomorrow

In a corner, a brave squirrel hides,
With acorns piled high, it boldly resides.
The kitchen's a jungle of leftover pies,
As the fork and spoon dance in hungry surprise.

A cat on the counter pretends to be king,
Surveying his realm like a pampered old thing.
Dogs roll in sock piles, tails wagging like mad,
While the laundry room's become a circus, quite bad!

The curtain's a stage for the fading sun's light,
As shadows play tag—oh, what a delight!
Mom's secret stash is just out of reach,
While dad's in the recliner, the remote is his speech.

So laughter echoes from room to room,
In the wacky dance of life's joyful bloom.
With each little mishap, a giggle takes flight,
In this cozy abode, all wrongs feel quite right.

Gathering Stars

In the attic, a hat flies high,
Chasing the dust, like a curious spy.
Sparkles of laughter drift through the cracks,
As socks dance together, plotting their tracks.

A broom with a broomstick, they take to the sky,
Whisking up memories, oh me, oh my!
Jars filled with giggles line up on the shelf,
While we concoct plans to outsmart ourselves.

The Aroma of Possibility

In the kitchen, mischief brews in a pot,
Spices stir laughter, believe it or not.
Cookies are giggling, pies join the cheer,
As flour throws a snowball, it's that time of year.

But watch out for pancakes, they flip and they fly,
Chasing syrup rivers, oh my, oh my!
The smell of the fun whisks us away,
To places where smiles are the price we pay.

The Glow of Goodness

A lamp hums a tune, casting shadows so bright,
While chairs join a conga, all ready to bite.
The floorboards creak out a jolly old song,
As pillows giggle, they can't wait too long.

The mirror winks back with a cheeky delight,
Reflecting the joy that dances at night.
With glow of farce, each corner ignites,
This place is a circus with all its delights.

Spinning Threads of Light

In the den, little spools weave stories anew,
While a cat on a cushion dreams of the view.
Curtains sway softly, gossiping low,
As colors blend bright, putting on a show.

The clock does a jig, while moments collide,
In patterns of laughter, we lovingly bide.
With friendship the fabric, stitched tight and true,
Each thread tells a tale, just waiting for you.

The Hearth of Togetherness

In the kitchen, we all collide,
Pasta splatters, laughter can't hide.
Mom's dance moves, quite the show,
Dad trips over a rogue step, oh no!

Cookies burn, smoke fills the air,
Grandma swears; it's quite a scare.
Yet in the chaos, smiles gleam bright,
This messy love is pure delight.

Stitching Light into the Fabric

Needles jab, and threads unwind,
Mismatched patterns, oh so kind.
Stitch by stitch, we sew our dreams,
Laughter echoes, or so it seems.

A patchwork quilt with stories to tell,
Of sock monsters and trampoline fell.
In every square, a giggle sewn tight,
Each fabric whispering joy and light.

Whispers of Tomorrow

Fortress of blankets, pillows stacked high,
Whispers of secrets, laughter that flies.
Allies in darkness, shadows of play,
Guardians of dreams, twilight's ballet.

Plans for the morning, pancakes galore,
But first, a battle of who'll snore more.
Tickles and giggles, the night won't dim,
Adventures await, on a whimsical whim.

Foundations of Light

Building blocks, a towering mess,
Squeals of delight, it's a hilarious test.
Dad's big toe meets the castle's gate,
Oh dear, the cries of 'Please, just wait!'

With each topple, we laugh and shout,
Constructing memories, no doubt about.
This playful space, oh so bright,
Home of laughter, warmth, and light.

Sunbeams Through the Blinds

Dust bunnies dance in the light,
Sunbeams tickle, oh what a sight.
Cats plot mischief, they've made a plan,
Fish in their bowl? They're part of the clan.

Socks on the floor, a colorful mess,
Each step a joy, sometimes distress.
Sunshine giggles, the curtains sway,
In this wild playground, we laugh and play.

Paths of Unity

In the kitchen, we stir up a cheer,
Mixing the batter, bringing us near.
Flour on noses, we're all a delight,
Cakes fall apart, but spirits take flight.

Silly old games, we giggle and tease,
In our togetherness, we feel the ease.
Maps of the past, with routes that we've roamed,
Every lost path now feels like home.

The Comfort of Familiarity

The couch is a throne, we all claim a seat,
With popcorn explosions and snacks to repeat.
Squirrels outside, share stories of lore,
Every glance exchanged means there's always more.

Laundry piles high, a colorful wall,
Each missing sock tells a tale, after all.
The kettle whistles a playful tune,
In our cozy chaos, we're over the moon.

Breezes of Resilience

Open the windows to let giggles fly,
The breeze carries joy, like clouds in the sky.
With every small mishap, we wave it away,
Our laughter is powerful—it brightens the day.

Rain might come knocking, a surprise from above,
But we dance in the puddles, all soaked with love.
So bring on the storms, we'll weather the test,
In this whirlwind of life, we're lucky and blessed.

Sheltering Clouds

Beneath the ceiling, laughter soars,
As dreams collide with open doors.
A cat in a hat seeks a throne,
Claiming each cushion as its own.

The fridge hums a symphony bright,
Dancing shadows in the soft light.
A sock puppet war starts by the chair,
While Grandma's cookies vanish in midair.

The walls do giggle, they softly sway,
Holding secrets of each sunny day.
A crack in the plaster, a cheeky face,
Winking and plotting in this snug space.

The Garden of Belief

In the backyard where daisies bloom,
Whimsical gnomes hold a party in the gloom.
A worm in a top hat leads a parade,
While ants breakdance on a picnic laid.

The flowers gossip of the bees' last flight,
Chasing butterflies, from morning till night.
A scarecrow dreams of a life on the stage,
Plotting his act from a yellowing page.

Rainbows sprout from the garden hose,
With laughter and giggles in every rose.
Sunflowers nod as they sway in tune,
Hoping to catch a glimmer of the moon.

Walls that Embrace

These sturdy walls hold tales galore,
Of pizza nights and snacks galore.
A skateboard ramp made of dad's best chair,
Imagine the joy, the wild flair!

Each nook has a memory, bright and bold,
From battles fought with toys of old.
The wallpaper peels with a chuckle and grin,
As tiny mischief hides deep within.

A closet full of laughter and fright,
Where shadows play tricks in the night.
The echo of giggles, the brimming cheer,
Walls hug the folly that draws us near.

Seeds of Tomorrow

A jar on the shelf holds wishes and dreams,
Growing wild like fantastical beams.
Crayons and markers, a colorful mess,
Sketching the future, we're more than blessed.

In this safe haven, we craft with glee,
Imagining worlds for you and me.
With giggles that bubble and whispers that cheer,
The seeds of tomorrow are planted here.

A paper airplane sails past the door,
Charting a course to adventures galore.
With each little laugh, with every smirk,
Hope grows like magic, with love as the work.

A Tapestry of Aspirations

In the living room, dreams stretch wide,
Socks mismatched, the laundry's our guide.
Coffee spills, what a glorious mess,
Life's clumsy dance, we must confess.

Pancakes flip in a flashy way,
Chasing the cat, they twirl and sway.
Unmade beds tell stories untold,
In this circus of love, bright and bold.

Crayons on walls, a masterpiece made,
Kiddo's giggles echo, never fade.
A treasure map drawn on the floor,
Adventure awaits just behind the door.

As laughter spills into every nook,
Life's a recipe, come take a look.
Imperfect moments woven with cheer,
In our patchwork of hope, let's persevere.

The Embrace of Evening

As twilight settles, the dinner's a sight,
Pasta's a sculpture, but oh, what a fright!
Salad's a mountain, dressing cascades,
Who knew a meal could cause such charades?

Candles flicker, while Uncle Joe sings,
Voice of a frog, with imagined wings.
The dog joins in, barking his part,
In this symphony, we all play a heart.

Board games erupt like balloons in the sky,
Monopoly madness, oh me, oh my!
Lost in the rules, we dive right in,
With laughter and mischief, nobody can win.

Evening wraps us in a cozy embrace,
Spilled wine on the couch? Just part of the race.
Under this roof, joy and chaos blend,
In this riot of love, we'll never pretend.

Windows to the Heart

Through the kitchen window, the cat makes a leap,
Chasing its shadow, in a playful sweep.
Dishes piled high, a mountainous sight,
Whiskers twitching, oh what a delight!

Pajamas all day, what a fun way to thrive,
Neighbors peek in, just to check if we're alive.
Jugs of juice, splattering like rain,
In this carnival, there's always a gain.

Baking cookies, measuring by eye,
Oops, too much flour; how did that fly?
With chocolate smudged on our silly cheeks,
These moments, they're golden, not for the weeks.

Our windows frame laughter, stories, and cheer,
In this quirky abode, there's nothing to fear.
Come look through and see; the heart beats here,
In this merry chaos, we hold love dear.

Parables of the Past

Old photographs line the crooked shelf,
Memories giggle when taken by self.
Grandma's recipes, a dash of fun,
Cooking disasters, each meal's a pun.

Stories of socks lost in the wash,
Legends of gingerbread gone to a posh.
Each squeaky toy, a witness in time,
The echoes of laughter, our favorite rhyme.

Tales of adventures on a rainy day,
Building a fort, where shadows could play.
Mom's hair a wild nest, a crown in the mist,
She'd declare, "Darlings, remember this twist!"

Inspired by antics, our past becomes light,
Each twist in the tale, a reason to write.
In the pages we turn, may joy always last,
For love in our home is forever steadfast.

The Echoing Heartbeat

In the corner, socks take flight,
Chasing dust bunnies 'til night.
They twirl and leap, a wild parade,
Stirring laughter where dreams are made.

Naps on couches, a cat's loud snore,
Chips and dip spill on the floor.
Echoes of giggles, a playful fight,
All the chaos feels just right.

Cookies burn, smoke alarms sing,
Family dance-offs—a silly fling.
The clock ticks fast, yet time stands still,
Every moment, a thrill to fill.

Under the roof, joy bounces free,
Collecting laughter like candy, you see.
As mismatched socks find their pair,
Home is the heart, brimming with care.

Tapestries of Shared Dreams

In the attic, treasures lie,
A wobbly chair and a rubber pie.
Grandma's hat from days of yore,
Worn by kids who ran, then swore!

Each corner tells a tale of glee,
Of pillow fights and spilled iced tea.
A tapestry stitched with love so bright,
Every yarn spun feels just right.

Silly hats and mismatched shoes,
Exploring the world with silly views.
Bread and butter on every plate,
The taste of joy we celebrate.

Laughter echoes down the hall,
As memories unravel, one and all.
With every twist, they find their way,
In this dance of hearts, we play.

Places Where Shadows Dance

In the corners, shadows play,
Whispering secrets, come what may.
A monster under the bed at night,
Turns out, it's just a sock's delight.

The kitchen sees a rogue cupcake,
But who will eat it—Oh, the mistake!
Giggling kids in a tangle of legs,
Round and round the table, like little pegs.

Lighthearted whispers under the stair,
All the dreams coat the midnight air.
Each shadow twirls in a joyous trance,
In this rhythm, everyone gets a chance.

Home's a circus, with giggles loud,
Where even the furniture feels so proud.
In every flicker and flash of light,
Even shadows know, it feels so right.

Momentary Gardens of Joy

In the window, a pot of thyme,
Tickles noses, but I lose track of time.
Bees tickle flowers in laughter's burst,
Wilting hopes are quenched by thirst.

Sprouts leap from old, say "We're alive!"
Bouncing beans, they love to thrive.
A parade of blooms with silly names,
In any contest, they win the games.

Raindrops dribble from laughing leaves,
In this garden, nothing deceives.
Spinning sunbeams, a tasty treat,
Where every joy feels so complete.

Whimsical moments in every clump,
A giggling bird upon a stump.
These fleeting dreams sprout and play,
In gardens of joy, we find our way.

A Symphony of Possibilities

In the kitchen, pots do dance,
While spoons take their chance to prance.
The fridge hums a funny tune,
As leftovers plot a cheeky swoon.

The living room's filled with socks galore,
Each hiding from the laundry war.
Cushions giggle with playful grace,
As pets leap through the cozy space.

In corners, dust bunnies convene,
Planning their next big unseen scene.
With a tickle here, and a poke right there,
It's a circus ride without a care.

So raise a glass of fizzy cheer,
To the silly joys that linger here.
For every giggle that we may find,
Sparks a symphony of the best kind.

Rooms of Resurgence

In the hallway, echoes of cheer,
Where squeaky shoes bring joy near.
Walls dressed in colors bright and bold,
Whisper secrets of laughter told.

The bathroom's a splashy paradise,
With rubber duckies and a wink so nice.
Toothpaste battles and soap-sud splashes,
Turn mundane moments into flashes.

The study holds wisdom in heaps,
While books conspire, secrets it keeps.
But the chair starts to yawn, feeling tired,
From all the tales that it's inspired.

Every room's a canvas unique,
Where silliness lights up the mystique.
Creating bursts of laughter and glee,
In these spaces where we feel free.

The Heartbeat of Solace

A sofa that knows your favorite spot,
Gives hugs that tie you up in knots.
Fluffy pillows with big, bright eyes,
Assist you in your quest for surprise.

A cat on the windowsill, a watchful guard,
Surveying the world, ever so hard.
With a flip and a flop, it takes a leap,
And down goes a plant – oh, what a heap!

The echo of laughter fills each room,
While dust dances, giving gloom a zoom.
And in the quiet, a tickle remains,
Of moments shared where joy sustains.

In this space, the heart beats fair,
In sync with giggles and love in the air.
A testament to the fun and delight,
That fills our days from morning to night.

Lanterns of Laughter

In the corners, shadows play a game,
As lanterns flicker with their flame.
Every chuckle brightens the room,
Like fireflies chasing away the gloom.

The dining table, a feast for all,
Where stories and puns rise and fall.
With every bite, a joke takes flight,
Turning mere meals into pure delight.

The bathroom mirrors hold their glee,
Reflecting the antics of you and me.
Each splash of water, a giggling tune,
As rubber ducks join the afternoon.

So let the lanterns illuminate our way,
Through absurd moments that brighten our day.
With laughter as our guiding light,
We weave through life's delightful night.

The Sound of Hope

In the kitchen, pots decide to dance,
Spoons jump high with a rhythmic prance.
The toaster sings a burnt-toast song,
Even the fridge hums all day long.

Laughter bounces off the walls so bright,
Echoes of joy bring a comic light.
The vacuum cleaner's a howling wolf,
Chasing dust bunnies, it's a playful gulf.

The clock ticks in a zany beat,
Tick-tock, tick-tock, it can't be beat.
Even the cat joins the funny parade,
Sliding on floors, it's a big charade.

At dusk, the noises fade, it's true,
But a giddy hush replaces the view.
With memories of laughter, here we cope,
In every creak, a whisper of hope.

A Bough of Blessings

A tree in the corner with fruits of cheer,
Gives apples of laughter and oranges of beer.
Bananas stretch and giggle with glee,
Saying, 'Come on, climb, you silly bee!'

The branches sway, tickling the walls,
While squirrels dance, having no falls.
A nest of chirps, not a worry at all,
Funny little feathery friends at the call.

Leaves whisper secrets, a wild fun game,
As each one shouts, 'No two are the same!'
What blessings we gather from fruit and from leaf,
In this silly tree of joy, beyond belief.

A bough of giggles is what we behold,
With stories of laughter that never grows old.
Gather 'round, revelers, it's time to share,
In the shade of this tree, joy fills the air.

The Colors of Kindness

Crayon rainbows spill across the floor,
Dancing in colors - they help us explore.
A purple chair laughs with a polka dot grin,
While a yellow wall hums, 'Let the fun begin!'

Blue curtains flutter like butterflies bold,
Telling tales of kindness, a sight to behold.
A green rug is a stage for a plucky chair,
It's auditioning for laughs, if you care!

Orange lamps giggle, casting warm light,
While pink pillows shout, 'Stay up all night!'
Such vibrant kindness swirls here and there,
In this quirky abode, there's love everywhere.

So grab a brush, let your thoughts fly free,
In this canvas of kindness, come paint with me.
With every stroke, the laughter grows wide,
In the colors of kindness, we all abide.

Dreams in Every Corner

In every nook, a dream takes flight,
Mice on a bicycle zooming past night.
A teddy bear holds a secret parade,
While socks on a line form a colorful charade.

The old armchair tells stories untold,
With cushions of laughter, both soft and bold.
A lamp with a winking light in its eye,
Chimes in with giggles as time goes by.

Potted plants chatter of adventures bizarre,
As they plot their escape to the twinkling star.
With every twist and each playful turn,
In corners of joy, there are dreams that burn.

So let us lay in this dream-filled space,
Chasing the giggles, time can't erase.
With dreams in our hearts and laughter in store,
In every corner, joy knocks at the door.

The Aura of Acceptance

In a room where the socks never match,
And the cat plays the role of a couch potato,
We laugh as we find a pie in the batch,
And wonder if it's friendly or just plateaus.

The blender hums like a jazz guitar,
While the dishes are stacked in a daring height,
An impromptu party, no need for a car,
As we all dance around the pizza sprite.

Bubbles float from a bath with no end,
Rubber ducks bounce in delightful glee,
Laughter erupts as we try to pretend,
That kitchen disasters were simply meant to be.

And when night falls, the stars shine through,
On a couch where we unwind with a snack,
In this chaos, love finds its view,
Mixing joy with the laughter we stack.

Chambers of Compassion

In a hall where chaos finds kindred song,
Each misplaced shoe tells a tale so grand,
We embrace the mess, where we all belong,
And even the laundry is never quite planned.

Here's to the microwave's quirky beep,
That signals dinner at just the right time,
We giggle and tease, no need to be deep,
As cereal becomes the gourmet sublime.

The fridge may sigh with rebellious rage,
A door that creaks like an old movie reel,
But within these walls, there's love on every page,
And laughter spins strong like a whimsical wheel.

Under blankets piled, we dream and unite,
With pillows that squabble for their own throne,
In this kingdom of humor, the mood feels just right,
'Cause here's where we cherish the joy we have known.

The Pathway to Bliss

On a carpet where crumbs hold their sway,
Every step is a crunch, a delightful surprise,
We follow the trail, come what may,
As dust bunnies gather to share their wise.

The coffee pot gurgles, a morning parade,
With mugs that have stories, chipped yet so bright,
As we laugh over plans that have long since delayed,
And toast to the chaos that feels so just right.

In the nooks where old puzzles gather their dust,
We uncover the laughter beneath all that pain,
Each piece tells a joke in the midst of the rust,
And we revel in humor like sunshine in rain.

As the day fades away with a warm, gentle glow,
We gather our tales, both silly and true,
In this dance of existence, together we sow,
The seeds of joy that are nurtured by you.

Radiance in the Gloom

In corners where shadows cautiously tread,
We paint the walls with colors so loud,
An oven timer beeps, a joy to be fed,
While the pets conspire beneath their proud shroud.

A sock puppet stage springs to life with a cheer,
As we juggle the chaos with giggles galore,
With mismatched ideas, it's all perfectly clear,
That our home is a stage we all can explore.

The vacuum roars like a pet in a fight,
While crumbs dance in circles around our feet,
We laugh at our plight, oh, what a delight,
As the couch becomes safe for all that we eat.

In the glow of the chaos, our spirits take flight,
We toast marshmallows to stories we weave,
In a world made of laughter, sorrow takes flight,
And the gloom turns to magic we gladly believe.

Whispers Beneath the Roof

In the attic, ghosts play cards,
The cat pretends to be a guard.
A sock puppet gives a speech,
While the mouse offers a peach.

Chairs argue over who's the best,
The fridge just hums, it needs its rest.
Dust bunnies dance, a wild ballet,
While the broom just stares all day.

Cups gossip about last night's brew,
The spoons think they're a fancy crew.
Together they plan a great escape,
But the cat's in charge, there's no debate.

A chandelier sways with delight,
As the cupboard sings into the night.
This quirky house knows how to play,
With laughter echoing all the way.

Lighthouses of the Heart

The toaster pops like a lighthouse beam,
A slice of bread, fulfilling a dream.
The blender stirs up a wild affair,
As milk and fruit float in mid-air.

The sofa declares it's the best seat,
While the rug rolls and dances its beat.
Pots clank for a party tonight,
The spoons wear hats, it's quite a sight.

A picture frame wiggles with glee,
Reminiscing of days by the sea.
Each photo a tale of love and cheer,
Making moments forever dear.

The windows wink at the passing breeze,
While the curtains sway with such ease.
Here joy and laughter never part,
In this merry lighthouse of the heart.

Dreams Nestled in Shadows

In the corner, old dreams doze,
Huddled tight like little crows.
The lamp shade whispers secrets low,
As curtains watch the shadows grow.

A clock chuckles, minutes dance,
Each tick a chance, a silly romance.
The dust gathers for a grand parade,
With the broom quite dismayed and delayed.

A book with pages stuck together,
Wants to travel, rain or weather.
While the chair tells tales of yore,
Of sock puppets and mystery lore.

The cobwebs spin a story of fun,
A world where socks can run and run.
In the depths where mischief lies,
Laughter echoes, touching the skies.

The Garden of Wishes

In the kitchen, pots bloom like flowers,
Spices sprout through sunny hours.
A wishbone sits, plotting its fate,
While the kettle plays 'guess the date.'

Lemonade flows like a river wide,
Glasses giggle, oh what a ride!
The blender hums a joyful tune,
As cupcakes dream of a grand afternoon.

The cookie jar, a treasure chest,
Holds sweet delights, oh what a quest!
The sugar bowl sprinkles cheer,
Together they craft the best of years.

This quirky garden of laughter blooms,
With half-crazed dreams and sugary fumes.
Every dish made with a heart so bold,
In this garden, wishes unfold.

A Watercolor Sky

A canvas draped in shades of cheer,
Where dreams float freely, flickered here.
The walls giggle with colors so bright,
As laughter dances, a pure delight.

The ceiling sweeps with clouds that sway,
Tickling thoughts that leap and play.
A sunbeam whispers, "Don't take it slow!"
While paint drips laughter, an endless show.

In corners, brushes lay in stacks,
Combing colors, like furry wacks.
Spilling secrets through splashes bold,
As stories of joy are splashed and rolled.

In this space, confusion is fun,
With each misstep, creativity's spun.
So here we cherish each silly sigh,
In the watercolor of a giggling sky.

Embracing Shadows

In corners dance the shades of night,
Their wobbly winks are quite the sight.
They wear capes made of dust and dreams,
Plotting mischief with silent screams.

One shadow trips, begins to roll,
An impish rogue with a wobbly soul.
With giggles echoing through the soles,
As chairs and rugs become their goals.

They twirl and flutter, embrace the light,
Conducting their frolic like a silly fight.
Each inch of gloom holds glimmers of jest,
In this mysterious, mischievous fest.

So let them whirl in the evening glow,
As we join the dance, moving to and fro.
Through laughter, we witness their grand charade,
In a circus of shadows, where dreams are made.

The Quiet Sanctuary

A nook where whispers gently sway,
With comfy chairs that love to play.
Where teacups shield secrets like a guard,
And silence giggles, not trying too hard.

The shelves hold tales of giggly lore,
Of kittens that dance and tigers that snore.
Each dust mote twirls like a cheeky sprite,
As shadows sneak in, cloaked in twilight.

The clock ticks softly, but laughs abound,
As time takes tumbles, turning around.
A cozy blanket steals the show,
With riddles woven in every row.

So we toast to silence with cups up high,
As the laughter echoes, oh me, oh my!
In this snug embrace, we find our style,
And jest with the universe, all the while.

Reflections in Stillness

In mirrors giggle with soft delight,
While echoes bounce in absurd flight.
Each glance reveals a joyful prank,
As humor winks from the bathroom sink.

The tiles wear smiles, slick and wide,
While puddles plot to drift and slide.
Socks perform acrobatics galore,
In the haven where silliness soars.

The faucet hums a tune so sweet,
As bubbles pop in a soft retreat.
With rubber ducks acting out their parts,
In this quiet world of whimsical arts.

So here we muse by the shimmering view,
Where laughter's wrapped in an endless hue.
In reflections that shimmer with glee,
We find our joy, wild and free.

Echoes of Grace

In a nook where laughter bounces,
And socks convene for secret dances,
We hum a tune, a playful cheer,
As dust bunnies twirl without fear.

A dog with dreams of being a cat,
Wears a hat and pretends to chat.
The goldfish boasts of deep-sea kings,
While the hamster practices his flings.

Life stirs in corners, with giggles tucked,
Beneath its weight, no hope is plucked.
The blender whirs a symphony raw,
As spoons form bands, it's quite the show!

So raise a glass of fizzy luck,
Here's to joy and all its muck!
We gather 'round in messy bliss,
For in this chaos, we find our kiss.

Nurturing Dreams

In a garden where the cookie crumbs,
Compete with dreams of dancing drums,
We plant our thoughts in flower pots,
Watered with giggles, not forgot.

Pillow forts are castles grand,
Where silly dragons take their stand.
A family feud over the last slice,
Becomes a contest of who's more nice.

The fridge hums tunes of midnight snacks,
As we concoct inventive hacks.
Leftover pizza, a gourmet treat,
Served on napkins, our fastest feat.

So let the curtains sway and spin,
For in our shenanigans, we win!
With dreams like kites, we twist and twirl,
In our world of whimsy, joy will unfurl.

The Hearth of Resilience

In the heart, where chaos meets delight,
Banana peels become a funny sight.
Spaghetti flings through the air like darts,
As laughter erupts from the wildest hearts.

The couch is a ship sailing through time,
With mismatched socks that dare to climb.
Dust settles thick, a cozy cloak,
As whispers of daydreams gently poke.

When the clock struggles, and time moves slow,
We spark up games, let laughter flow.
A dance-off breaks out with no rules,
Hippos and llamas, we're all just fools!

So gather 'round, with snacks in hand,
Here in our fortress, we make our stand.
Through all the grumbles and goofy strife,
Our hearth shines bright, celebrating life.

Lanterns on the Windowsill

A lantern flickers, shadows prance,
As the cat leads the nightly dance.
With mismatched lamps and silly hats,
We toast to nights and playful chats.

The fish are judges, swimming wise,
As we embark on our wacky tries.
Home-cooked dishes mysteriously float,
While leftovers play "guess the goat."

Blenders roar like lions at play,
While dishes pile, a colorful array.
Here, every mess is a badge we wear,
Crafting stories, without a care.

So shine your lights, let laughter beam,
In this quirky life, we live the dream.
Lanterns warm our hearts, we insist,
In the joy of these moments, none missed.

Hearthstone Reflections

In the kitchen, the pots play jigs,
While the spoons dance with joy.
The cat's on the counter, big and fat,
Claiming ownership—oh, what a ploy!

Chairs gossip softly, their legs creak loud,
As shadows dance on the walls.
The fridge hums a tune, offbeat and proud,
Inviting midnight snack brawls.

Laughter spills from the living room's glow,
Where socks wage war on the floor.
The dog dreams of bones, in a comical show,
While the goldfish gives an encore.

When the clock strikes twelve, the madness begins,
As dreams float like bubbles afloat.
In this haven of quirks, where silliness wins,
Home is a merry little boat.

Echoes of Tomorrow's Light

In the hallway, echoes play tricks,
Walls whisper jokes of the past.
The picture frames wobble, some do the splits,
As laughter and memories clash vast.

The laundry room's a circus, I'm sure,
Where socks disappear in thin air.
Finding matches is more than a chore,
It's a hunt beyond compare!

The sun peeks in like a cat on a ledge,
Casting shadows that wiggle and cheer.
Each corner knows secrets, they tease and allege,
Making everyday life seem more dear.

Living here, the future arrives with a grin,
Painting dreams with colors so bright.
The echoes of laughter are where it begins,
In this circus of love and delight.

Safe Harbor for the Soul

The couch holds stories, both old and new,
Where the cushions conspire with glee.
Each crinkle a giggle, and one, maybe two,
In this nook of familial spree.

The kitchen's like magic, a chef's grand stage,
Where flour flies with a comedic flair.
The oven's a joker, it seems quite sage,
Baking potatoes that swing through the air!

And outside the window, the world rushes by,
But here time dances in a waltz.
Watching troubles sail like leaves in the sky,
We learn to laugh at our faults.

This harbor of warmth, like a hug on the run,
Reminds us that joy always stays.
Through each little quirk, every pun and pun,
We find comfort in humorous ways.

The Room of Unspoken Stories

In a corner, the broom leans with a frown,
Tired of hiding the dust.
The plants exchange gossip; they never back down,
While the lamp plays peekaboo, just because!

The window frames carry a few smudged tales,
Of raindrops that danced on the sill.
As each sunset winked and laughter prevails,
This place is a treasure, quite shrill.

The books on the shelf wear coats of surprise,
Their pages flip funny little rhymes.
Cushions debate about who's the most wise,
While the clock chimes in playful chimes.

In this room, the silence speaks loud,
Where every shadow is a friend.
In the silliness here, I take an unbowed,
For every story with laughter shall blend.

The Pillars of Tomorrow

In the corner sits a chair,
With a cat that rules the air.
It surveys all with a smug grin,
As if to say, "Let the games begin!"

The fridge hums a silly tune,
While socks dance under the moon.
The dust bunnies plot to escape,
Making plans in their fluffy drape.

Laughter echoes off the walls,
As a pizza box takes a fall.
The dog thinks it's all a game,
Chasing crumbs, it's never the same!

Under the stairs, secrets hide,
A treasure chest, a burst of pride.
With toys and dreams in disarray,
The past returns to join the fray.

Stories Beneath the Roof

Under the table, stories lie,
Of the last time, we tried to fly.
A rocket made of chairs and sheets,
Launched us off our little seats!

Grandma's tales of ghosts and ghouls,
All while we played our silly fools.
With every twist and every turn,
A new adventure was our yearn.

The laundry sings a squeaky song,
As clothes go tumbling, rolling along.
Each sock has a story to tell,
Of mishaps in the laundry well.

And on the walls, drawings bright,
Reveal our imaginations' flight.
The crayon scribbles, wild and free,
Tell of the fun we shared with glee.

The Solace of Silence

In the quiet, socks start to chat,
Mapping routes for a game of pat.
The fridge kicks off a whispered tale,
While the curtains sway, the softest veil.

A cup of tea just spills its dreams,
Dancing droplets in gentle streams.
The kettle whistles a quirky tune,
Join us, it says, we'll talk till noon!

The clock ticks slowly, trying to tease,
As dust motes swirl like happy bees.
Each second's laughter, a little joke,
In the sanctuary where silliness spoke.

A pillow fight, oh what a scene,
With feathers flying, bright and keen.
The silence breaks in joyful shouts,
In our cozy nest, fun never pouts.

Hummingbird Whispers

In the garden, whispers bloom,
Hummingbirds zip, dispelling gloom.
They chat about the sweetest flowers,
While we gossip in sunlit hours.

The fountain splashes a comic hit,
As ducks waddle, their dance a skit.
Each quack is filled with fun and cheer,
Inviting all to gather near.

Among the pots and old clay stains,
A raccoon jokes about its gains.
Beneath this roof of humor spread,
Every giggle wraps us like a thread.

With leaves that rustle tales so bright,
And sunbeams flickering with delight,
Here in this space, we laugh and sway,
While hummingbirds carry our cares away.

The Spirit of Togetherness

In the kitchen, pots do cha-cha,
While the cat plays expert salsa.
We dance like it's a grand parade,
Chasing laughter, being unafraid.

Grandpa tells his jokes from dawn,
While the plants pretend to yawn.
Suddenly, the toaster pops,
And we all burst into hops!

Together we bake a giant pie,
It's so lopsided, oh my, oh my!
We share stories with crumbs on our face,
Every mishap feels like a race.

In this chaos, joy finds its way,
With every blunder, we choose to stay.
Life is better when we all unite,
In our quirky home, everything's right.

A Quilt of Memories

Patchwork of stories, sewn with glee,
Each square a tale, shared with tea.
Missed stitches, but who really cares?
Laughter connects like magical flares.

A grandmother's sock tucked in a seam,
Her wild tales, like blueberry cream.
Uncles fighting over the last bite,
While cousins giggle with pure delight.

Finger painting splashes from last year's fest,
Our creative chaos is truly the best.
Socks mismatched, but hearts on the same thread,
In our colorful quilt, joy's widespread.

Each sleepless night, a story to unfold,
In this whimsical fabric, memories hold.
Through every snip and sew, we find,
Laughter threads that bind us, heart and mind.

Breezes of Change

The curtains flutter like a butterfly,
As we debate who can bake the best pie.
Flour flies, and then the laughter spills,
Even the fridge joins in with its chills.

Who knew a broom could dance so fine?
We sweep up crumbs, we sip on sunshine.
The dog joins in, twirls around the chair,
Every corner's filled with jubilant flair.

A sudden chill from the bathroom door,
Reminds us why we all love the floor.
With socks as our slippers, we skate and slide,
Navigating joys we simply can't hide.

Whispers of change fill the air today,
As our silly antics lift spirits to play.
Through breezes and giggles, we find our song,
Together in chaos, we joyfully belong.

Reflections Beyond the Mirror

In the glass, we see a silly crew,
With toothpaste mustaches and hair askew.
Who's that dancing with mismatched socks?
Oh wait, it's Dad, pulling off his socks!

Mirror reflections host a big show,
As we dance with our shadows, putting on a glow.
Mom twirls around, knocking over a vase,
And suddenly the room's a wild, happy place.

The mirror cracks with laughter so loud,
We can't help but smile, we're feeling proud.
Every goofy pose and silly grin,
Shows the essence of joy lying within.

Beyond the glass, we find pure delight,
As we embrace the chaos and share the light.
In this playful world where laughter is dear,
Reflections of joy bring our hearts near.

The Heart's Embrace

In the corner sits a chair,
A cat who thinks he's quite the heir.
He rules the room with lazy grace,
Demanding snacks with just one face.

A lamp that's flickering, old and bright,
Seems to argue with the fridge at night.
They bicker softly, a comical plight,
In a dance of shadows, a goofy sight.

The couch is filled with forgotten crumbs,
From joyful nights and silly hums.
A treasure map for hungry mice,
Who think these crumbs are worth a price.

In this space where laughter blooms,
Even the vacuum hums happy tunes.
It's a circus filled with giggles and cheer,
Where every day's a wacky frontier.

Rays of Renewal

The sun peeks in through dusty blinds,
Awakening hopes and silly minds.
A pot on the stove, whistling away,
Promises soup for a rainy day.

The plants on the sill, in utter dismay,
Are convinced they've got something to say.
They gossip loudly with leaves so green,
About that one time they got quite the sheen.

The fridge is a treasure, though slightly stale,
With leftovers dressed in a mismatched tale.
Each container's a time capsule, truly bizarre,
Like a soup from last August, a culinary star.

Laughter bubbles like a pot that won't quit,
As socks disappear, can you believe it?
In this light, every mishap's a show,
Rays of laughter bring warmth as they flow.

Echoes from the Hearth

The fireplace crackles with tales of old,
But truly, it's just the logs getting bold.
They whisper secrets, then glow with pride,
Over the charred remnants of marshmallows fried.

A clock on the wall ticks out of time,
Chiming away with a silly chime.
"Five o'clock somewhere!" it often proclaims,
While the teapot steams, fighting its flames.

The wall art giggles, on hung-up display,
As if they know all, yet choose to play.
Each crooked frame, a jokester's touch,
Raising questions like, "Why this much?"

In this theatre of warmth and fun,
Where moments of joy have just begun.
Echoes of laughter fill every nook,
As we dance through life like a storybook.

Timeless Threnody

In the attic, the old toys reminisce,
Pondering days they surely miss.
A doll with a smile, slightly askew,
Wonders why no one plays peekaboo.

The board games stacked like a leaning tower,
Challenge the dust with unyielding power.
A game of life, but who's keeping score?
Maybe the cat, as he sprawls on the floor.

The old piano plays a tune so rare,
Notes flutter out like a feathered prayer.
Despite the missed keys and offbeat clunks,
It's the kind of music that simply shrugs and funks.

In this realm where oddities thrive,
Nothing really ends, we just come alive.
A timeless threnody, quirky and bright,
Turns every wrong note into pure delight.

Threads of Aspiration

In a corner where dreams collide,
Socks unmatched take a wild ride.
Toasters sing with golden cheer,
While the fridge whispers, "Get outta here!"

A dance-off with the vacuum's might,
Cereal whispers secrets each night.
Curtains sway as cats conspire,
In the realm where hopes never tire.

Mugs stack up, a tower so grand,
Each one holding a quirky brand.
The couch gives a sigh, soft and round,
As laughter echoes all around.

In this space, every quirk's a thrill,
As we scribble dreams with a coffee spill.
Laughter's the paint that colors our day,
In a place where hope likes to play.

A Sanctuary for Stars

A pillow fort that reaches the sky,
Where imagination dares to fly.
Cardboard rockets blast off with glee,
As aliens sip on sugary tea.

The rug spins tales in colorful hues,
Of adventures we wish to choose.
Squeaky toys are our best pals,
As we plot to outsmart mom's yells.

Our laughter bubbles, a fizzy sound,
As we ride on the giggles we've found.
Walls listen close, with grins in their seams,
Holding tight to our boldest dreams.

At dusk, the stars peek through the blinds,
Whispering secrets only hope finds.
In this haven, the fun never ends,
Where imagination leaps and bends.

Walls that Hear Our Prayers

The walls grumble like old, wise friends,
Hiding laughter where the laughter ends.
Sticky notes flutter, plans to devise,
As the dog plots to steal the prize.

Dinner's a circus, a culinary show,
With spaghetti tossed like confetti snow.
The cat judges with a regal stare,
While crumbs scatter, showing we care.

Echoes of giggles bounce out the door,
And the floors dance on a wooden floor.
In every nook, a story unfolds,
As the scent of popcorn brightly holds.

The walls may listen with bright, eager ears,
Collecting our hopes, our unspoken fears.
Their laughter joins ours in a merry refrain,
Where every chaos is part of the game.

Beneath the Comforting Eaves

Under the eaves where the shadows play,
The gnomes have a party on a rainy day.
Sock puppets dance in a wacky parade,
While the teapot whistles a serenade.

The picture frames smile with stories to share,
As the dust bunnies spin in carefree air.
Everything's quirky, not quite divine,
But in this space, it's perfectly fine.

The lightbulbs flicker like fireflies bright,
As we conjure up dreams in the soft twilight.
Chairs gossip of secrets they know,
As popcorn kernels put on a show.

In the corners, our laughter's the paint,
As happiness lives without any constraint.
Together we weave a tapestry rare,
In this shelter, fanciful and fair.

The Threshold of Possibilities

Step through the door, what do we see?
A cat with a hat, as proud as can be!
Chasing its tail with utmost delight,
While the fridge hums softly, flickering light.

A sock on the wall and a spoon on the chair,
The dog makes a pillow from the dust in the air.
The couch is a portal to lands of pure bliss,
Where dreams turn to giggles and laughter's the miss.

The hallway's a runway for fashion's best heroes,
With laundry as gowns, and slippers like zeroes.
Each corner a canvas of sketches and dreams,
Where silly and serious twine at the seams.

Every crack in the wall tells stories untold,
Of tears turned to chuckles as life unfolds.
So let's raise a toast with cups filled with cheer,
To the wild, wacky moments that bring us near!

Notes from the Attic

Up in the attic, where time seems to pause,
Dust bunnies are dancing and laughing because,
An old rocking chair creaks a tune that's so nice,
While cobwebs spin tales that are spicy like rice.

A trunk filled with treasures from days gone by,
A hat that was worn by dear Uncle Kai.
Each item a laugh, a giggle or two,
As the old broom just sways, "Come share this with you!"

Ghosts of good stories drift in through the beams,
Whispering secrets and far-off dreams.
With a tattered old map where X marks the spot,
For a treasure of laughter—who knew we had that?

Each box a surprise, each creak a delight,
A symphony playing on this dusty night.
So we'll scribble some notes on the memories grand,
And dance with our shadows, each step carefully planned.

Silence of Sown Seeds

Beneath the old floorboards, a whisper does stir,
Seeds of laughter sprout up, don't you dare concur!
With every step taken, they giggle and quake,
As the curtains sway gently, a playful wake.

A seedling of laughter takes root in the hall,
While charades of the squirrels are heard through the wall.
The sunlight creeps in, tickling shadows awake,
With vines of joy climbing every mistake.

In corners where silence is meant to reside,
The echoes of snickers can't be denied.
They tumble and tumble till glee fills the air,
A garden of cackles that none can compare.

So here in this silence, we plant with great cheer,
Awaiting the harvest of laughter so clear.
Let's water these moments with love and with grace,
As we grow in our joy, we can't help but embrace!

Radiance in the Quiet

In the quiet of night, where shadows do play,
The laugh of a mouse steals the hush of the day.
A light bulb flickers, tells jokes on the side,
While a book on the shelf tries not to collide.

With a teapot that whistles just out of tune,
And spoons that play symphonies under the moon.
A tapestry woven from laughter and dreams,
In a room where the quiet is bursting at seams.

Mirrors winking back, they wink with a grin,
Reflecting the joys that are waiting within.
Each creak in the floorboard, a whisper, a song,
Reminding us all, this is where we belong.

As the clock ticks away, it can't help but smirk,
For the magic of moments is where we all lurk.
In the solace of stillness, we'll find our own light,
Radiance glowing, making everything right!

The Resilient Rose

In a pot that's cracked and worn,
A flower grew, all hope not shorn.
It waved its petals in the air,
Saying, "I'm here—please do beware!"

With dirt on the floor and stains on the wall,
The sun shone bright, giving it a call.
"Forget what they say, I'm not just a weed!"
"I'll bloom where I want, that's my kind of creed!"

I watered it once, that proved to be fun,
Now it dances to tunes; oh, what a run!
With laughter it greets all who pass by,
"Come sniff my scent, or at least say hi!"

So here's to the blooms that shine with glee,
In homes filled with chaos, it's joyful, you see.
They laugh at the dust and sparkle like stars,
Reminding us all, we can heal our scars.

Blossoms of Possibility

Amidst the clutter, a sprout appeared,
A little green thing, though mostly smeared.
It said, "Oh, I'm late, but here I am now,
In the land of the socks and the dishes—oh wow!"

With an ardent spirit under layers of grime,
It chuckled aloud, "Wait, is this my time?"
"Among dust bunnies, I'm king of the spring,
My throne's a shoebox—let the fun begin!"

In this quirky realm, where the oddities dwell,
It tells silly stories of garden and smell.
"Let's dance in the kitchen, throw spices up high!
And bake up a storm—hey, who let the cat spy?"

So here's to the odd ones that sprout with delight,
In homes filled with laughter; they shine extra bright.
For blossoms of beauty come in every form,
Even tangled with mismatched socks as their norm.

Gates of Gratitude

Knock, knock, who's there? A joke to unfold!
Behind the door, warmth and laughter untold.
"Come peek at the treasures, the clutter, the fun,
A family of chaos, still shining like sun!"

With pots in the sink and kids running wild,
A magical place where every heart's styled.
"Thank you for crayons—I made quite a mess!
And that bowl full of flour? Just a small guess!"

The windows are fogged with too many smiles,
"Hey, open the fridge! Surprise! More than miles!"
Each door holds a memory, each room a tale—
Of toys and of stories, of rain and of hail.

So here's to the laughter, the hugs that we share,
To thankful hearts finding joy everywhere.
For roaming through life, there's always a gate,
Where gratitude blooms, and it's never too late!

Dreams on the Dusk

At twilight's hour, when the day's gone to rest,
A flicker of hope gives each room a quest.
"Hey there, sleepyhead, don't snore just yet!
There's magic in dreams, I'm not finished yet!"

In the corner sits a chair, teetering proud,
With stories to tell to the sleepy night crowd.
"Oh, let me weave tales of gnomes and their hats,
And cats that can dance, oh my, imagine that!"

As shadows stretch long and the giggles unfold,
Far from the mundane, young dreams take hold.
"We'll fly like balloon boats on clouds made of cream,
While parents just mutter, 'They're lost in a dream!'"

So here's to the dusk, where dreams come alive,
In homes filled with laughter, we always thrive.
For in each whispered wish and fun-filled report,
Lies a spark of pure joy—our hearts to support.

The Melody of Moments

In the kitchen, pasta spins,
A dance of noodles that never wins.
The cat's on the counter, feeling bold,
Snatching the spoon, quite uncontrolled.

Laughter erupts when the toast goes pop,
Out flies the jam with a funny plop.
We dodge and we weave, like a game of tag,
Two slices later, we're starting to brag.

The fridge hums sweetly a tuneful rhyme,
Telling us we're just wasting time.
Yet here we are, our humor so bright,
With every mishap, we dance through the night.

In the living room, the movies play,
But popcorn's just staging a wild ballet.
We laugh till it hurts, and the couch starts to sag,
A symphony of joy, nothing to brag!

Vignettes of Victory

A sock on the floor sings its lonely tune,
While the dog's eyeing treats like a cartoon.
We cheer for blunders, each mishap's a win,
As flour goes flying from my prancing kin.

The vacuum's a monster that dances and weaves,
Chasing our shadows as everyone leaves.
We rally together, a family of jest,
With sneakers and giggles, we're truly the best.

In battles of board games, the stakes hit the roof,
While Grandpa cheats slyly—now that's the truth!
With laughter as currency, we fill up our bank,
In this wacky world, we consider ourselves rank.

So raise up your glasses filled with sweet cheer,
In this silly saga, we hold each other near.
Vignettes of our lives etched silly and bright,
With love in the air, every day's pure delight!

The Existing Echoes

Echoes of laughter bounce off the walls,
While mismatched socks are having their balls.
In corners, the dust bunnies form a new gang,
Planning a coup, oh, the mischief they sang!

Grandma's old chair creaks with a giggle,
Telling us stories, it loves to wiggle.
Every creak, a promise, a quest so grand,
From tea parties held in a world so unplanned.

The mirror reflects all the silly faces,
Trying on outfits from strange time and places.
Our cat gives a sigh, judging our style,
As we spin and twirl in a makeshift aisle.

The echoes of moments replay in delight,
Every blunder, a treasure, so perfectly right.
Around every corner, surprises abound,
In our joyful ruckus, true happiness found!

Embracing the Unseen

In the attic, we sift through memories bright,
Where the dust grins wide in soft golden light.
A hat from the '70s with feathers and flair,
We wear it with laughter, pretending to care.

The fridge hums a tune, but its door's a tease,
Plenty to nibble, who knew? What a breeze!
We find half-eaten cake, a sugary swipe,
Low on the calories, still high on the hype.

Pajamas our armor, we battle the day,
With giggles and grunts, come what may.
In pillow forts tall, we build our own throne,
For kings and queens crafting laughs of our own.

With friends gathered round in this whimsical scene,
We create memories full of silly sheen.
Embracing the laughter, the glee, and the fun,
In every little moment, our hearts weigh a ton!

The Portrait of Possible Futures

A cat sits on the chair, dreaming wide,
While the dog plots a heist, oh what a ride!
Forks are dancing, spoons in a race,
Kitchen chaos, but we all embrace.

Chasing dust bunnies, we somewhat thrive,
Mom calls it cleaning, we call it a jive.
The fridge hums tunes like a jazzy band,
Food fights are afoot, life is oh so grand!

Laughter spills over furniture like tea,
Mismatched socks dancing with glee.
Movies play in a spaghetti pot,
In this wild circus, worries are shot!

So paint the walls with stories you're told,
In this riot of color, life's bright and bold.
Where futures seem possible, bright as the moon,
All share the stage in a silly cartoon!

Windows to New Beginnings

Peeking out the window, what do we see?
A squirrel in a top hat singing with glee.
Birds in a choir, with worms playing bass,
This morning's meditation is a humorous chase.

A breeze whispers secrets through cracks in the glass,
Carrying rubber duckies that float right past.
Why did the chicken cross? A new gig awaits,
Singing along, with our knock-knock plates!

Ice cream for breakfast, why not take a chance?
Rainbow sprinkles make any sadness dance.
Behind every curtain, a joke's waiting there,
In this realm of laughter, we lighten our care.

So open those windows, let laughter pour in,
No room for frowns, let the joy begin.
Each day a new canvas, a blank, cheerful book,
Here's to the whimsies that life undertook!

A Quilt of Kindness

Stitches of laughter woven with care,
A patchwork of memories, it's quite the affair.
Each square a story, a giggle, a sigh,
Grandma's knitting needles are flying high.

We toss in our dreams like confetti afloat,
Spinning wild yarns on a sentimental boat.
Tickle the seams with a wit so divine,
Stitching up warmth with a splash of sunshine.

At the corner of laughter, a trouble spot waits,
Where a monkey in pajamas tries to fix plates.
Fluffy tales and marshmallows stuck on the side,
There's no judgment here, only joy to abide.

So gather 'round closely, let kindness spread wide,
In this glorious patch, we'll wear joy with pride.
A quilt of hilarity under bright, goofy skies,
In warmth and in laughter, true comfort lies!

The Embrace of Tender Moments

In a blanket fort, we hold court for the day,
Dressed as pirates, we set sail away.
Pillow fights echo like thunderous roars,
With giggles and tickles, we create open doors.

A dance with the fridge, oh what a delight,
Magnet chess pieces in a daring fight.
We twirl and we spin with our grandest moves,
While broccoli pirates show us their grooves.

The clock spins around, time's having a ball,
Every tick-tock reminds us of it all.
We treasure the whispers of secrets well kept,
As mom makes the cocoa, and the kitten has crept.

So cherish these moments, both silly and sweet,
In the embrace of laughter, life's journey's complete.
Here's to the hugs, the quirks, and the giggles,
In each tiny snapshot, our joy simply wiggles!

The Bridge to Tomorrow

In a house where dreams run wild,
Laughter echoes, light and mild.
A bridge to tomorrow, built on cheer,
With socks on the floor and no sign of fear.

The kitchen's a treasure, crumbs galore,
Where cookies dance on the kitchen floor.
A dog in a hat sings a silly tune,
While the cat plays bass with a light of the moon.

Grandma tells tales of her youth so bright,
With a wink and a nudge, she captures the night.
The chandelier swings as the jokes unfold,
In this bridge, the spirit never grows old.

So here's to the antics that make us glee,
To unexpected moments of pure jubilee.
Hand in hand, we smile and we sway,
Building a bridge that won't fade away.

A Tune of Renewal

In our cozy nook, a tune drifts around,
Where laughter is found, and joy can be crowned.
The toaster's a drummer, the kettle's a flute,
Together they play, oh what a hoot!

The couch is a stage for the kids' silly cries,
As they perform magic with bright, gleaming eyes.
An umbrella stands guard like a knight on a shelf,
Who knew a household could entertain itself?

A dance in the kitchen, we all take a turn,
As the spaghetti noodles twist and we yearn.
To catch the sweet moments, so fresh and so bright,
A melody made from love and delight.

With socks on our heads, we laugh and we spin,
As the cat walks the runway, proud of her kin.
In this tune of renewal, we thrive and we play,
Creating rhythms to chase blues away.

Nestled in Trust

Nestled in trust, where silliness thrives,
We wear mismatched socks and practice our jives.
A chair's become throned for the pet with a crown,
While we giggle and joke, never wearing a frown.

Sheep on the walls, and frogs on the floor,
Make the home feel like a playful chore.
A pancake with eyes that can blink and can dance,
And the fridge hums a tune when we give it a glance.

A game of charades with the dog as our host,
As he barks out commands, giving all of us a boast.
With laughter as sunlight and silliness as rain,
In this nest of delight, there's much to gain.

So let's hold onto laughter, keep it close like a hug,
With glee in our hearts, we'll dance like a bug.
With friends and with family, we'll never feel rust,
In the comfort we share, forever we trust.

Petals of Positivity

Sprinkled like petals, our giggles unfold,
In a garden of joy, more precious than gold.
We water our dreams with bright, silly games,
As laughter erupts, calling out all our names.

A cat on a skateboard, what a wild sight!
With a smirk and a wink, it rolls with pure fright.
The walls hum with stories of whimsy and cheer,
As the smell of fresh cookies brings everyone near.

Oh, how we dance through the echoes of cheer,
With our quirks on display, there's nothing to fear.
In the petals of positivity, we delight in the now,
With joy as our anthem, we take a bow.

So gather together, let laughter ignite,
In this colorful space, oh, what a sight!
With memories blooming, we weave our own art,
In the garden of giggles, we share from the heart.

Whispers of Contentment

In corners where laughter sneaks,
The cat's got secrets, it never speaks.
Dust bunnies dance in a merry jig,
Remind us all, life's quite big.

The fridge hums low, a gentle tune,
Leftovers plotting a grand monsoon.
Coffee cups stacked like a little hill,
Each sip a promise, a cozy thrill.

Mismatched socks find a joyful pair,
While sponges gossip without a care.
Potted plants gossip of sunshine dreams,
In their leafy whispers, laughter beams.

Glances exchanged with a wink and a grin,
Even the laundry feels like a win.
In this quirky space we call our own,
Joy hums softly, a playful tone.

A Sphere of Promise

Balloons float high, a colorful plot,
The dog chases shadows, in a scruffy spot.
Children's toys spill like a vibrant stream,
In this chaos, we chase our dream.

The clock ticks funny, but we're never late,
With ice cream spills as our dinner plate.
Giggles erupt from a pillow fight,
A world of wonder in the soft moonlight.

Fridge magnets are poets, crafting lines,
While we share stories 'neath twinkly signs.
Pajamas worn proudly with a silly flair,
Creating memories hanging in the air.

Amid mismatched spoons and socks galore,
Every corner whispers, we can't ignore.
In this gathering swirl of jolly intent,
Life's a sweet circus, a merry event.

Brightening the Shadows

In the creaky old chair, stories unfold,
Ghosts of the past with a glimmer of gold.
A potted cactus, a prickly friend,
With optimism blooming that won't bend.

The shelves hold treasures, odd and bizarre,
An old rubber chicken, a broken guitar.
We dance in the kitchen to tunes that we play,
Mixing joy with flavors in an odd ballet.

A mirror that squeaks with each honest look,
Reflects our mischief, like a fun storybook.
And the shadows that linger behind the couch,
Wink at the laughter, not an angry grouch.

Each corner glimmers with happiness spun,
In this place, even chores can be fun.
As the sun sets low and the laughter swells,
We beckon the night, where whimsy dwells.

Harbor of Serenity

The kettle whistles a merry tune,
While socks share tales of a sunny noon.
Teacups clink like friends in disguise,
As we savor moments beneath soft skies.

The couch, a ship on a sea of dreams,
Where giggles float and happiness beams.
A cat naps lightly on a pile of hats,
While the world spins gently, no need for chats.

Cookies vanish in a blink of an eye,
As crumbs become treasures for ants passing by.
We parade around in our ninja attire,
Chasing giggles like a whimsical fire.

Even the cracks in the walls have a laugh,
Worn and beloved, they tell stories by half.
In this harbor, where all's thought through,
Harmony sails with skies ever blue.

A Mosaic of Promises

In the corner, a cat takes a nap,
Dreaming of fish and a grand Snap!
While the dog plots his next big scheme,
To steal the sandwich—it's not a dream!

The lamp flickers, a light-hearted dance,
Making shadows that prance and prance,
Mom yells, 'Please don't jump on the chair!'
While Dad pretends he just doesn't care.

Kids are giggling, a treasure map drawn,
To find the snack stash, they're never wrong!
Glowing with laughs, in this chaos bright,
Where every mishap brings such delight.

Bubbles float from the washing machine,
Like mini-aliens, all shiny and clean,
The plants eavesdrop, in pots they conspire,
For a slice of cake—or maybe a flyer!

Roots Reaching Upward

The plant on the shelf thinks it's a tree,
Stretching its leaves, so wild and free.
Saying, "Look at me, I'm reaching the sun!"
While the cactus rolls its eyes—what fun!

Under the couch, a sock leads a crew,
Team Messy Socks, with a mission so true.
To rescue all mates from the depths below,
And put on a dance show—don't you know?

Dad still thinks the vacuum's a beast,
Chasing him down for its lunchtime feast.
Mom just chuckles, with a wink of her eye,
"Next time, dear husband, just let it fly!"

The fridge hums a tune of creamy delight,
While leftovers wiggle, all ready for night.
Every door squeaks, it joins in the fun,
When laughter's the fuel, we all weigh a ton!

The Canvas of Comfort

On the wall hangs a portrait, a sight to behold,
Of Grandma dancing—oh, so bold!
Pet goldfish cheer in their watery ball,
And wonder, is Grandma the best of them all?

The couch throws a party of cushions galore,
Each with a secret, a soft-hearted lore.
While the TV hums the latest prank trend,
A sitcom of chaos, that'll never end.

In the kitchen, pots clatter their tune,
Trying to cook up a dish with a swoon.
"Too much spice!" the cook laughs and sighs,
As smoke signals rise, to the heavens they fly.

Under the table, toys scatter and play,
While jigsaw puzzles all look the other way.
In the land of comfort, laughter's in bloom,
Where every mishap brings joy to the room!

Tides of Tranquility

In a bathtub, with bubbles quite high,
Sailboats made of soap drift by.
Rubber ducks quack as they chat about dreams,
Of floating to beaches with ice cream streams.

In the yard, squirrels plot their next snack,
While the sun paints the grass like a friendly track.
Mom shouts for quiet, but the wind sings loud,
A chorus of giggles from the mischievous crowd.

The clock ticks away, a rhythmic dance,
Tickling the moments that barely get a chance.
While shadows stretch long over the green,
In this tranquil place, we're all seen serene.

With a cuddle in blankets, and laughter to share,
Every heartbeat echoes, like a gentle prayer.
In life's sweet embrace, let the joy rush in,
For tides of tranquility will always begin!

Lanterns in the Hallway

A flickering light in the dark,
Chasing shadows, playing a spark.
I told my socks to find their mates,
They slipped away, leaving just fates.

The broom took a dance on the floor,
While the dust bunnies planned to soar.
And in the laughter, we twirl and slip,
With every stumble, the joy we grip.

So let the lanterns guide our way,
Through mischief and games we laugh and play.
With snacks stacked high and giggles wide,
In every corner, our hopes abide.

The hallway hums with playful cheer,
As whispers of joy fill the atmosphere.
Amidst the chaos, we giggle and tease,
In our little world, we do as we please.

Coziness in the Chaos

The couch has seen better days,
But we snuggle up in a jumble of rays.
Popcorn rains from the ceiling above,
As we argue who's really in love.

Blankets vie for the best quilted throne,
While the cat claims the seat as its own.
The coffee cups dance, the mugs do twirl,
In this cozy chaos, we give it a whirl.

Games scattered like leaves in the breeze,
Amidst the laughter, we find rare ease.
A pillow fight breaks out with flair,
Fluffy warriors in the air!

We bask in the mess and all the absurd,
With every mishap, a silly word.
In pandemonium, we find our way,
Coziness thrives where chaos will play.

The Chorus of Resilience

In a house where laughter sings,
And dishes dance on invisible strings.
The dog barks a beat to our cheer,
While the cat rolls by, too cool to care.

We build castles from pillows high,
As we plot and scheme, our spirits fly.
The walls sigh joy, a happy refrain,
In silliness, we embrace our grain.

The fridge hums sweet whispers at night,
Of leftovers dreaming of morning's delight.
We chase our dreams in mismatched socks,
Resilience blooms, it never locks.

Through fumbles and spills, we hold our ground,
In our quirky rhythm, magic is found.
This joyful chorus sings loud and free,
In persistence, we find unity.

Heartbeats in Hidden Corners

In nooks where giggles softly swell,
And whispers of dreams weave a spell.
The clock ticks loud with a silly tune,
As shadows dance beneath the moon.

Jars full of smiles line up on a shelf,
Sharing secrets of the child within self.
We trip on laughter, fall into grace,
In every stumble, we find our place.

Beneath the table, a paint-splashed crew,
With crayons at war, in colors so true.
The heartbeats echo, pure and light,
In every corner, joy takes flight.

From tangled wires and bricks askew,
A tapestry of dreams, stitched anew.
In hidden corners where we find glee,
Life is a riddle, and love is the key.

www.ingramcontent.com/pod-product-compliance
Lightning Source LLC
Chambersburg PA
CBHW070002300426
43661CB00141B/133